Timothy B. Merriman

THE ITEMIZATION OF TIME

Timothy B. Merriman

THE ITEMIZATION OF TIME

According to [The Holy] Scripture and Prophecy
From Adam to the first Second Temple Desolation

(The Condensed Version)

The First Step to Truly Understanding why "Jesus Christ" has not returned... Yet!

TIMOTHY B. MERRIMAN

Timothy B. Merriman

THE ITEMIZATION OF TIME (According to Scripture and Prophecy)
Copyright © 2020 by Timothy B. Merriman
Richfield, NC 28137   U.S.A. All rights reserved.

Except for the use of brief quotations in a book review and certain other noncommercial uses that are permitted by Copyright Law, no part of the contents of this book or covers of this book may be reproduced in any form or used in any manner whatsoever without permission in writing from the author or the express written consent of the Publisher.

This book was printed in the United States of America. All rights reserved under International Copyright Law. First Printing, 2020

ISBN: 978-1-7331889-7-5 Print
ISBN: 978-1-7331889-5-1 eBook

DEDICATION

This book is dedicated to my "SIX" (That's Right – SIX) loving daughters, Gwen, Lois, Philadelphia, Julia, Jennifer and Grace; but especially to my Lois and to my Jennifer. To Lois who was born with a rare chromosome deficiency and lived only nine years; because Lois showed me how to fight and be courageous and happy – no matter what life throws at you. Had she survived, Lois would have been twenty and nine years of age as of the year 2019. To my Jennifer because she showed me how to be content and thankful with even the simplest of things that life offered to her. I never saw her upset over anything. In fall 2014 Jennifer became a victim of murder through Domestic violence – when her bother-in-law gunned her down in cold blood. Jennifer was seventeen. I would be remiss if I did not mention my wife Andrea in my dedication. With the tragic loss of our daughter Jennifer, Andrea is determined not to let Jennifer's life become a forgotten statistic in the long tragic history of domestic violence; nor, if she has anything to do with it, any of those in similarly dangerous situations, be without their own voice and the opportunity for

H.E.L.P. *(Hope, Empowerment, Life-skills and Prevention), her comprehensive support program offered through the advocacy of* <u>***Feminine Life Rebuilders***</u>*; the non-profit organization Andrea has founded. Andrea has shown me how to turn pain and anger into power and purpose. Believe me when I say that the ability to do so helps out a lot – especially when faith is the writing subject. I thank YHWH for all my girls; especially those two who I can no longer hold and tell them how much I love them. Lastly, my Eloah forbid me – if that in any way, I should fail to show Gwen, Philadelphia, Julia and Grace, the four daughters YHWH has left for me to treasure, how much they have meant to my continuous mental and spiritual wellness over all of these following years after our family's two tragedies.* <u>*Saying*</u>*,* <u>***"Thank you girls!"***</u> <u>*is not enough*</u>*. I pray that YHWH continue to richly bless you according to his own will and purpose; because I am persuaded that nothing else could be more rewarding or could give you any more Joy and Holy Confidence as we see the coming day of Messiah's return approaching.*

The Itemization of Time

Timothy B. Merriman

_H.E.L.P._

Feminine Life Rebuilders

Feminine Life Rebuilders (FLR) is a registered 501 (c) (3) organization. Any and all of additional contributions you will be inspired to give are entirely tax-deductible. Feminine Life Rebuilders is a means by which we all can help in their effort, so that many of the victims of domestic violence will always be remembered and that great voice of domestic violence survivors will be heard and never silenced in fear and shame again. FLR extends, "H.E.L.P." to facilitate programs that offer Hope, Empowerment, Life skills and Prevention methods to women by design - *young and older*. Nevertheless - There are inclusions clauses that are set in place with FLR; which are dedicated to offering help and support for those that might be members of the LGBTQ-IA communities. FLR works with their local state (N.C.) community partners as well as advocates in other state areas to find programs, services and safe shelter for all of their domestic violence sisters in need. You can and we encourage you to do so – visit the FLR site at: www.feminineliferebuilders.org. See what they are all about. Then make a donation. It will go a long way towards services to survivors and those at risk. This may include classes, training workshops, or funds needed to get to safety.

Author Contact Information:

Timothy B. Merriman
PO Box 231
Richfield, NC 28137–0231

Email Address:

dayandhourministry@gmail.com

Timothy B. Merriman

*Unless otherwise indicated, all Scripture quotations contained in this booklet are taken from the *King James Version* of the Holy Bible.

**Some scriptural references in this book may be referenced in paraphrased form – however, the location of the reference itself is also listed for verification, accuracy and the readers' own study.

***Internet addresses (blogs, websites, etc.) and contact information such as telephone numbers and addresses given in this book are offered as resources. They are not intended in any way to be or to imply an endorsement by this book's author and its publisher; nor does the aforementioned vouch for the contents of these addresses, sites and numbers for the life of this book. As with all meaningful endeavors or considerations; due diligence is the sole responsibility of the individual. Proceed with caution.

Cover:www.flickr.com/photos/jerusalemprayerteam/8636513963/in/photolist. Cover adaptation: Timothy B. Merriman

The Itemization of Time

Table of Content

Dedication VII

H.E.L.P. X

1) Introduction 1

2) The Itemization of Time 12

3) From Adam to the Flood 20

4) From Shem to Egypt 25

5) From Egypt to Kings 30

6) From Kings to Babylon 38

7) The Babylonian Captivity 46

8) Seventy Weeks Prophecy 51

9) The BC/AD Corresponding Chart 58

10) What Happens Next? 66

References 79

Who is Timothy B. Merriman? (*Continued from back page*) **83-81**

The Itemization of Time

CHAPTER 1

INTRODUCTION

Shall we cut to the chase? We start off with "**The Hypothesis**," "**There is a GOD**." How long has *intellectual* man inhabited the earth since his creation? Is asking "*God*" for an answer to that question; asking him too much? And, if man has been on the earth for so long; is there some **_expressed ordained time limit_** to his existence here on this earth, as an organic species – by this mysterious "*God*?" Naturally throughout our history, before the written languages, oral traditions have preserved our days and years in this earth, religiously - *if you'll excuse the expression.* Once man's written languages became the preeminent method for preserving histories, man has tried to keep all things in his social ways of life alive and fresh in their easier to preserve forms of words. So – how did man's years seemingly get lost or at the least, mixed up in time?

Some say man has been here for a mere 6000 years. Others have made guesstimate claims man has been here for the better part of 6 million years (humanorigins.si.edu). What is the truth? Can it be proven by faith from the Holy Bible? Before we go too far, let me say two things clearly. <u>I believe there is a God</u>. <u>I believe the Holy Bible is the translated **WORD** of God</u>. And for <u>me</u>, <u>LIFE</u> is the undeniable proof that some type of "God" is out there somewhere – *in some unimaginable state* – existing somehow beyond time. Even though every person in religion feels ***their*** God is the only **True** God, and I am not an exception; for instructional purposes only, I will yield the floor *"somewhat"* to other religions, to agnostics and atheists. This entity or force may not be "my *God*." It may not be "your *God*." But, as far as our creation (*and we most certainly did not create ourselves*) IT/HE is the "God" of our creation nonetheless, end-period. And, we had better hope and pray IT/HE is lucid in spirit as we are and the Holy Bible is true when it declares, *"...is a rewarder of them that diligently seek him"* (Hebrews 11:6). Because – whether we are willing or not to acknowledge IT/HIM; he is our only hope for eternal life.

If you are one who is unsure, in regards to the existence of *"God"* or you are one who seriously dissents to religions and insist that there is no "God," at least at the intellectual level; then seriously consider this fact

The Itemization of Time

of our lives. With nuclear missiles at their helms and ready to be launched by allies and enemies alike, <u>and no matter how hard we might try to prevent them, likely in the future, if not already</u> - Jihadists and terrorists; it stands to reason no matter how long man has been here gracing the events of history, whether it has been for 6000 years or 6,000,000 years; it seems there has appeared through the possibility of worldwide Nuclear proliferation, yet another infallible fact. In light of such dark present, and even darker future developments; man's time is limited and it is running out faster than most of us would care to have to admit. For those who have no faith in "God" or <u>do not believe he even exists</u> (*God calls <u>them</u> fools*); how bright is your future beyond that unlikely event you will live to see 100 years of age? After you are dead and gone, was there any purpose to your life ever existing from the word go? Let us be honest here. If this earth is going to be destroyed by man; what purpose were our lives to begin with? And, if this world is to somehow continue; who will remember us ever living in 10,000 years or so? Then what will our lives have meant? What is your life when you are dead and anyone who is alive never knew you existed and no record on file acknowledges your presence in time? After we are dead, what good is philosophy and <u>religion</u> - <u>if it is all just made up</u>? You see, that is what many think concerning the concepts of God. Here is what one spiritually logical mind had to say concerning my religion and my faith in a Messiah, *"If in this life only we have hope in [Messiah], we are of all men most miserable"* (1st Corinthians 15:19). For those who do not believe in "*God*," what's next for them? For my peace, I never want to be intimate with what it is like to live and to die without "<u>HOPE</u>." Such an existence brethren, friends, associates and Satan's bamboozled ones, is the life of a fool.

However, if you do believe in the possibility of the existence of God, I have a whole new set of questions. Does God tell us how much time we have all together? And if he does, is there a way to find out how much of that time we have used up? Since it is supposed by so many that we all came from one set of parents (***Adam and Eve***), even with all of our wars, plagues and turmoil; one would think that keeping up with a universal time would have remained gravely relevant. So then, why is not the true revelation of what time it is a worldwide knowledge and understanding? I wanted to know all of those questions and many more that are asked along that same line. So, I read what many of those so-called Holy Bible experts had to say. I looked at what several of our vaunted biblical theological giants of yesterday had to say; and I readily listened to much of what many of today's popular so-called "televangelists," pastors and or otherwise great (*considered so by many in the mainstreams of modern*

The Itemization of Time

Christianity) Christian leaders, teachers or whatever title they tend to give themselves today, had to say. I looked ...and I read ...and I read ...and I looked some more. After I got tired of reading and looking for those things I felt had some semblance of truth or making any kind of reasonable sense; I recognized I was more confused after I began my so-called research and study than I was before I first started to look. I saw things; but I could not get my footing on enough solid spiritual ground to make heads or tails of what I felt I was seeing. Peering *"through a glass, darkly"* (1st Corinthians 14:12) would have been a big understatement.

In a moment of what I expect was Holy Spirit clarity, I realized something extraordinarily frightening. I concluded that most of the sources I referenced for my so-called, *"enlightenment¿"* did not actually believe the Holy Scriptures or its translated/transliterated versions (*Holy Bible*). I say it was a shocker for me, because in many instances the theologians were ready and willing to accept men's reports of history inside of their history books, over what many times the Scriptures - *from my perspective,* spoke to in clear and logical terms. To make a long story short (*condensed version*); I had to make a decision in regards to my new directions for research and study of time. I had to determine who I was going to believe, no matter what conclusion I came to. I know this may come as a shock to some. I chose to trust in God and what I believe is his translated WORD, the Holy Bible. I determined that the only time *I might* give man the opportunity to even give me the time of day, was when or if the Holy Scripture was *subject-silent*. I felt that was only fair. So long as it did not confuse the issue of *what time we are really in and how much time we have left*.

After I made that easy choice, my next issues were was the full chronology of years in the Bible to begin with? And if so, could I find them all? Literally, every one of the theological cites and sources I saw seemed to think the Bible did not posses such information and so did not have the ability to take the objective researcher chronologically from day one – all the way to the end of ordained time for all species of carbon kind. I would say they all agreed there was the beginning and there is an end. That was the real easy conclusion to arrive at. Especially when we consider that every living thing that mankind has had the opportunity to encounter and study in his realm is of a temporary nature. In other words all natural, physical, carbon based living things have their end date. Only thing is, just that most of the time; we do not know when that end date will come. Granted, there are many billions of people that are with the belief that they will never or can never truly end. Different strokes for different folks I suppose. Besides, I am sure there are many books already written that debate that controversial subject. So I doubt my comments will redress the issue. It is bad enough I must keep reminding myself this is a research and study as it relates to our true time accountability; up until the first desolation of the second temple in this book – ***and beyond to the end*** – with its full complement in my first primary publication, "**IT'S MUCH LATER THAN YOU THINK!**"

So, can the Holy Bible alone get us chronologically from day one in years to "**The End;**" without any historical gaps or theological gaffs? That is the thing I thought that I really wanted to know. I did not know if the theologians were right or not. They appeared to be quite confident. I really wanted to find out for myself. Many of you know the Holy Bible has many time dates and events to glean from. The question was did they connect in a continuous, coherent, countable and chronological line all the way to the end to that infamous Judgment Day? As I have said already, I wanted to know. In truth, I wanted to know if that voice I had been listening to for what I could say was around four years was, The Real Thing. Because about the time my spirit curiosity asked unorthodox questions, I began receiving what I can only describe as, "*extraordinary revelations*." What was being told to my spirit shook my soul. Next came that common mistake often made in carnal thinking. I asked myself a spiritual question. I asked, "Is this really **GOD** speaking to me?" Yeah I really did that. I am sure none of you guys have ever asked that ignorant question. We all should know it says in the Holy Bible, do not lean to our own understanding (Proverbs 3:5) and try the spirits by the Spirit (1st John 4:1). Albeit, in my opinion, I do not feel it was the question that was ignorant. It was the person that I was asking the question to - <u>Me</u>. In short, my answer to the question I had asked myself was replied back to me by me with yet another question, "How in this world would I know?" Look, I am not saying my new perspectives were unknown before my discernment. I just had never heard anyone address them according to the perspectives I had received. I certainly had not considered the new conclusions; which these new perspectives forced me to come to. All of their spiritually unsettling ramifications peculated in my head. So yes, I began to wonder. Is this *God*? It was at that time - *once I began to doubt* - my spiritual eyes began to get dim. I was going spiritually blind as it related to the matters I had not long before fervently asked *God* for insight regarding. <u>Take some advice. When you bump up against the spiritual walls of ignorance; do not ask yourself for answers.</u> I know this is *Bible Understanding 101* for most believers. Though it took me a minute or two, the words I just advised you with for your insight, I found to be just as critical for my own. I understand it is absolutely my reality when I say, "*I am not worthy of the least of all the mercies, and of all the truth, which thou hast showed unto thy servant;*" (Genesis 32:10).

The Itemization of Time

NOTES

Timothy B. Merriman

NOTES

The Itemization of Time

CHAPTER 2

THE ITEMIZATION OF TIME

In the spirit of desperation for truth, I asked YHWH, "Why cannot I see it? I am looking right at it. I know I am looking right at it. But, I simply cannot see it. I know it is there. But, I just cannot see it. I need for you to help me. Heal my eyes so that I might see! I will not see anything unless you have mercy on me, and show me." I said these words and much more. I said them in a bunch of different ways, but the bottom line was if YHWH did not show me, I would not see and I would be 100% deceived without a doubt. Not very long after - *in a matter of days I suppose* - I heard from heaven and YHWH continued on with his instructions to me. He asked me was I sure about all of the numbers? I said based on the instructions from the Holy Spirit I felt my heart was able to hear; my count should not be off, one year - *maybe*. Look, I'm

The Itemization of Time

just being real here people. YHWH instructed me to check and recheck the numbers. Maybe you missed something. So I did. Then he had me to check and recheck them again and again and again - so on and so on. I did so. It is like I said before, I was sure that everyone else's advanced counts were off. I simply did not know where the problems lay with my count. When I tried counting the way Bible pundits would have me to count; and I admit that I did take a stab at it - just in case. My accounting discrepancies just got even worse. After that hair-splitting experience, I retreated back to where the Spirit positioned me originally from the start. I guess YHWH let me do all of those restarts and redresses from my lack of understanding, to allow my spirit to confirm that I had left no stones unturned. So that the direction he was going to take me in and what he was about to show me was the only logical and reliable choice. YHWH asked me if I was content that all of the numbers accounting for the time of Adam were accurate. I said, "Yes." Next he asked me was I sure with the order of the numbers I used? I said yes. Not for YHWH and me, but to make sure you and I are on the same page, I am going to show you a rare treat. I am going to show you <u>my itemized listing</u> of **<u>All Biblical Time!</u>**

The opening you read is from the book, "**<u>IT'S MUCH LATER THAN YOU THINK!</u>**" That book claims all chronological biblical history and prophetic time is listed. This book takes the readers into AD 70 and the destruction of the second temple. This excerpt has the un-updated words, "**All Biblical Time**!" In part, this partial time listing is so the reader may get the flavor of the larger book; to perhaps determine in their own minds, if they would like to obtain the entirety of information in the larger publication. I suppose at this time – *in full disclosure* – I should take some time to clarify to everyone why that book and this information pertaining to it were written in the first place. The truth – I wanted to know if any man could know when the last day was and if that information could be known, would God reveal it to him. Look you guys. I know what the Holy Bible appears to say in no uncertain terms. I will cite it for you - right now. "<u>*But of that day and hour knoweth no man, no, not the angels of heaven, but my Father only*</u>" (Matthew 24:36). I have it on good authority though, when we read that passage alone and as is, we are not looking anywhere near as deep as we should; if we can see anything spiritual at all. With all of my many long-held beliefs and long-standing curiosities pertaining to the Holy Scripture, I decided - *if you will* - to believe God at one of his pledges. He said in what I trust is his Holy Word, "*If any…lack wisdom…ask…God* [who gives] *to all men liberally…and it shall be given him*" (James 1:5). And, Paul backs this up in a way, saying "*…that which may be known of God is manifest in* *them; for God hath showed it unto them*" (Romans 1:19-20). Since, I believe the Holy Bible; as far as I am able to understand it. I basically asked God two questions. Since he doesn't hold back on the part of wisdom; I asked him if the information of knowing "*the day and the hour*" can be known from him, would he give me **that** wisdom to understand when that day and hour would come. Really, I know some of you are scowling and have frowns on your faces right now. How could I ask such a question; when I know God is not going to answer me. You see! That is the kind of attitude the Bible is talking about. It says we have not because we ask not. (James 4:2) So I asked. Solomon asked for wisdom and received it. I believed just the opposite of what many of you are right now, believing in your hearts. You believe that no one can know! Though I uncertainly disagreed with your widely-held premise and theology; notwithstanding and in a compromise, I would meet you halfway on your debatable dogma. Maybe no one knows now, because no one has asked - lately! Or perhaps they just tried to figure it out by themselves. In my view, that is error. All that needed to be determined was if that information and understanding was knowledge and discernment that could be known from God. I thought that was fairly clear in its simplicity. So, like I said. I asked.

I have always had my suspicions that *God* had a millennial week

(*7000 years*) plan. So, I asked *God* would he help me go through the Holy Bible to find and account for every significant year leading up to that end. I asked him was all that time recorded inside the Bible. I mean really guys; I went way over the initial two questions that I originally told you I intended to ask. I have no doubt *God* understood. With the 7000 years now in the forefront of my mind, I wanted to set out on the journey – if *God* would allow and guide me. You already know I asked that. So, did I get an answer? Did I get the go ahead? Would *God* in fact, *accompany*, on my "*time*" journey; to come to whatever end I would? Can any man truly know the day and hour? The full book I wrote "<u>IT'S MUCH LATER THAN YOU THINK!</u>" answers all of the above questions and more. This booklet is only a sectional exert from that book and the spiritual aroma of things to come; should you decide to obtain the complete work of research and study to determine for yourself <u>*what time we are really in and how much time we have left*</u>. Also, if anybody should encounter controversy inside of this short, but revealing book of itemized time; I am confidence in my beliefs, it will be clarified in detail when you obtain the full complement in the core book. For now, take this short chronological walk from Adam to AD 70; then, after you acquire the full version - <u>to the beyond</u>!

The Itemization of Time

NOTES

NOTES

The Itemization of Time

CHAPTER 3

FROM ADAM TO THE FLOOD

Patriarch's Name	Age at son's birth	YHWH's Adamic Year	Ordained Time left
1) Adam created by YHWH Elohim		(1)	6000
2) Adam	(130) to Seth	(131)	5870
3) Seth	(105) to Enos	(236)	5765
4) Enos	(90) to Cainan	(326)	5675
5) Cainan	(70) to Mahalaleel	(396)	5605
6) Mahalaleel	(65) to Jared	(461)	5540
7) Jared	(162) to Enoch	(623)	5378
8) Enoch	(65) to Methuselah	(688)	5313
9) Methuselah	(187) to Lamech	(875)	5126
10) Lamech	(182) to Noah	(1057)	4944

The Itemization of Time

11) Noah ......(500) to Shem.......................(1557).......................4444

12) Noah (600) (100 - The Flood) ....(1657).......................4344

13) The flood.....(1 year)...........................(1658).......................4343
(Genesis 7:6-11 and Genesis 8:13-14)

Timothy B. Merriman

NOTES

The Itemization of Time

NOTES

Timothy B. Merriman

CHAPTER 4

FROM SHEM TO EGYPT
Shem's son Arphaxad is born 2 yrs after the flood (Genesis 11:10)

Patriarch's Name	Age at son's birth	YHWH's Adamic Year	Ordained Time left

14) Shem (103) (2) to Arphaxad...............(1660).......................4341

I have to judge this following section of the Messianic bloodline immediately after the flood, was sealed by Moses at the instruction of YHWH. They are now revealed in these last few minutes of prophetic time. The numbers you are about to see are the result from their unsealing. The process is revealed in the full book of time given and left in: <u>IT'S MUCH LATER THAN YOU THINK!</u>

15) Arphaxad (25) to Salah........................(1685).......................4316

16) Salah ....(30) to Eber.........................(1715).......................4286

17) Eber ....(26) to Peleg.........................(1741).......................4260

18) Peleg ....(30) to Reu ....(1771) 4230

19) Reu ....(28) to Serug.......................(1799) 4202

20) Serug .....(30) to Nahor....................(1829) 4172

21) Nahor ....(11) to Te′rah......................(1840) 4161

22) Te′rah ...(50) to Abram......................(1890) 4111

23) Abram ...(100) to Isaac ....(1990) 4011

24) Isaac ....(60) to Jacob.....................(2050) 3951

25) Jacob .....(130) to Egypt....................(2180) 3821

The Itemization of Time

NOTES

Timothy B. Merriman

NOTES

The Itemization of Time

CHAPTER 5

FROM EGYPT TO KINGS
(TO KINGS' NET YEARS)

While in Egypt, according to the witness of scripture, the Messianic bloodline by count is totally concealed from the Hebrew Scripture's historical records. So, biblical history seekers like me are forced to take other measures. My renewed efforts to continue the itemization of YHWH's time would emerge in the form of years passing by in the historical events of Israel and Judah (*Jews*).

Start Event	End Event	YHWH's Adamic Year	Ordained Time left
26) Slaves...(430) to freedom		(2610)	3391
27) Wilderness(40) to Promise Land		(2650)	3351

The Itemization of Time

"The time of the Judges"

(*As Deliverers of Israel*) Judges are in **bold type**.

From: Judges or Adversary	Yrs to Judges or Adversary	YHWH's Adamic Year	Ordained Time left
28) Chushan-rishathaim .(8) to **Othniel**		(2658)	3343
29) **Othniel** ....(40) to Eglon		(2698)	3303
30) Eglon ....(18) to **Ehud**		(2716)	3285
31) **Ehud** ....(80) to Jabin		(2796)	3205
32) Jabin ....(20) to **Deborah**		(2816)	3185
33) **Deborah** ....(40) to Midianites		(2856)	3145
34) Midianites ....(7) to **Gideon**		(2863)	3138
35) **Gideon** ....(40) to Abimelech		(2903)	3098
36) Abimelech ....(3) to **Tola**		(2906)	3095
37) **Tola** ....(23) to **Jair**		(2929)	3072
38) **Jair** ....(22) to Philistines		(2951)	3050
39) Philistines ....(18) to **Jephthah**		(2969)	3032
40) **Jephthah** ....(6) to **Ibzan**		(2975)	3026
41) **Ibzan** ....(7) to **Elon**		(2982)	3019
42) **Elon** ....(10) to **Abdon**		(2992)	3009
43) **Abdon** ....(8) to Philistines		(3000)	3001
44) Philistines ....(40) to **Sampson**		(3040)	2961

45) Sampson ....(20) End of Judges ....(3060) 2941

"End of Judges"

The period of the Judges ended in the fourteenth year of King David's reign. Date wise, it would be in YHWH's Adamic year of 3060 or 941 BC. Of course that date's landmark would be in the death of Sampson and arguably with the birth of the future king in Solomon. We must note this year in time because it is in our counting of time, what we call the beginning of the *net years* of kings. With our use of the term *net years*, we want everybody to recognize, we are referencing in our count of all ordained time, the numbers as they relate to the more important chronological accounting of the years. So, when we cited Judges ended; we were referencing that chronological count as it related to our count from the Holy Bible in this book. And, we were not implying that Israel no longer had judges; because indeed Israel did. As a matter of fact, the Jews unto this day still retain their branch in civil governance. Notwithstanding, with Israel's rejection of YHWH as their Adon and the establishment of the *"sovereign"* human kings, the role of the Judges would dissipate rapidly. Immediately thereafter, the Judges' symbol and influence as being Israel's backbone of hope, strength and wisdom, the defender and hero of the people would come to a close as long as Israel and Judah would occupy the Promised Land. How we came to our date

The Itemization of Time

in history is a bit sneaky, but truly uncomplicated mathematics. It is all explained in great detail inside of the greater book.

"Transition Complete"

Though there would never be any peace in David's reign as king; due to his, *"wayfaring"* behavior against Uriah (*A weaker low-ranking soldier in David's army*); when David committing adultery with Uriah's wife Bathsheba and later even being totally complicit with the cruel and merciless murder of Uriah himself. (2nd Samuel 12:1-**10**) We can state even with treason constantly lurking – *In David's son Absalom* – the concluding thirty years of David's reign would see Israel expand their territories and authority over their enemies still in their land. He would eventually get a new heart and a right spirit. (Psalms 51:10) Such a tender mercy from YHWH would enable David to endear the hearts and minds of the people in his kingdom. That bond would be a valuable tool in the coming years with the fulfillment of the prophecy against him by YHWH (*Because of Uriah and Bathsheba*); when inside corruption and conspiracy would temporarily rip away the kingdom from David's hands. Even so, with the birth of Solomon, David received in essence, the confirmation of YHWH's forgiveness. Solomon was that heir of David YHWH would come to love and honor as unified Israel's next and last king for the ages. Solomon's acceptance also solidified the events of that eventual redemption from the hands of Absalom and his heartbreaking treachery he would mount against David. Absalom was that temporary and would-be-king whom YHWH summarily rejected - but tolerated a few minutes for David's chastisement. Now let us refocus back on time.

It is YHWH's Adamic year of 3060 (941 BC). From the transition overlap of Judges and Kings, we have the kings' net years commencing with David's final twenty-six (26) years. Even though the kingdom of Israel was later, *"rent"* (1st Kings 11:29-37 & 14:8) from David's hand in the reign of Rehoboam (*His grandson*); then 307 years later, one tribe Naphtali was taken away as captives by king Tiglath-pileser of Assyria in 3367 (634 BC) and yet again later, in 3383 (618 BC) the rest of Israel was "*escorted*" to Assyria by then king Shalmaneser. From that end we are unable to continue to follow Israel in the accounting of time. But, let us not forget about the tribe of Judah. YHWH, in his mercy for David and His Holy City Jerusalem, left Judah in the land and in the hands of David's heir (*Grandson Rehoboam*). Because we have Judah's record; we are still able to count biblical time up through our history in the kings of Judah, up until Nebuchadnezzar.

Next is the "Net Years" of Kings

From Kings to Babylon

The Itemization of Time

NOTES

NOTES

The Itemization of Time

CHAPTER 6

FROM KINGS TO BABYLON

The "Kings of the United States of Israel" from year 3060 (*941 BC*)

The King	King's Successor	YHWH's Adamic Year	Ordained Time left
46) David	(26) to Solomon	(3086)	2915
47) Solomon	(40) to Rehoboam	(3126)	2875

"The Kingdom of Israel is taken from the House of David"

"The Kingdom is separated or divided" is often used to describe what happened to Israel after the reign of Solomon. However, the theology and notion behind the statement are false and misleading. In actuality, YHWH did not divide the Kingdom of Israel. My claim is only valid if one can believe the words of YHWH himself. "Thus saith the Lord, the God of Israel, Behold, I will rend [*slash, tear, rip*] the kingdom [*of Israel - the whole thing*] out of the hand of Solomon, and will give ten tribes to thee (*Jeroboam*): but he (*Rehoboam [Solomon's son]*) shall have **one tribe** for my servant David's sake and for Jerusalem's sake...)" (1st Kings 11:31-32). Recall now that Levites had no inheritance in the land. Levites are the physical priests of YHWH. YHWH is their inheritance,

> "...the Lord spake unto Aaron, Thou shalt have no inheritance in their land, neither shalt thou have any part among them: I am thy part and thine inheritance among the children of Israel...I have given the children of Levi all the tenth in Israel for an inheritance, for their service which they serve, even the service of the tabernacle of the congregation."
>
> (Numbers 18:20-21)

YHWH never actually separated the Kingdom of Israel. He merely left one tribe in Jerusalem for David and Jerusalem's sake. Judah (*Jews*) is not biblical Israel. They never have been and never will be. I do not say this disparagingly. I say it for divine bearing and bible study purposes. I must keep reminding people when I speak of Jews; I am not citing the Nation of Israel. That is not scripturally accurate. Maybe this disclosure will help others in their studies on Jewish heritage and the real Kingdom of Israel.

"The Kings of Judah to Babylon"

I have stated it before. Now I am saying it again. The records of the reigns of the kings of Israel and Judah were really meticulous and exhausting for me. When I read the records through Moses, the recorders and The Prophets, it was almost like I was trying to read them in three (3) dimensional writing and sometimes as this trilogy of dialects. Most of the time, when one king's reign was ending in one nation, another would continue in the other. It could get very confusing. The sister kingdoms kept tabs on each other as far as who was their brothers' leader. Far as the recorders were concerned it seemed, if one became king and was able to finish out the year – no matter when he started, it counted as a year for each king involved. Sometimes a king's son reign would overlap by years. Father King would hand over partial reins to his Son, while he helped him in transition over as the sole leader at the death of his father and old king. While my descriptive skills may be suffering here, the numbers are tight. After all, I did read them in 3-D. If I sense a need, I might use an initial to describe an event: i.e. <u>D</u> - death, <u>A</u> - assassinated, <u>ODK</u> - overlap & dual kings and <u>Ø</u> - means other. So let us start up again. Remember that we paused in the end of Solomon's reign at YHWH's Adamic year of 3126 or (875 BC).

The King **How long**	**Date of** **his years**	**YHWH's** **Adamic Year**	**Ordained** **Time left**
48) Rehoboam (17).......[3126-3143]..............(3143)................2858
49) Abijam (3)..............[3144-3146]..............(3146)................2855
50) Asa (41)..................[3146-3186]..............(3186)................2814

The Itemization of Time

51) Jehoshaphat (25-ODK)[3186-3210] ....(3210) 2789

--------------- 4 year overlap ---------------

52) Joram/Jehoram (8-ODK)[3207-3214] .....(3214) 2785

--------------- 2 year overlap ---------------

53) Ahaziah (1)............[3213-3214] ....(3214) 2785

54) Athaliah (6) ....[3214-3220] ....(3220) 2779
King Ahaziah's mother ruled Judah - A woman!

55) Jehoash (40-ODK) [3220-3259] ....(3259) 2740

--------------- 3 year overlap ---------------

56) Amaziah (29-A) ....[3257-3285] ....(3285) 2714

Amaziah's son <u>Uzziah</u> was only 4 years old at the time of Amaziah's assassination. Nevertheless, because he was the king's son, he was heir to the throne of Judah. He would likely be under tutors and whatever protection availed until such time he would ascend to the throne. Azariah finally began his reign at the age of 16.

57) Uzziah Azariah (52) [3297-3348]..............(3348) 2651

58) Jotham (16) ....[3349-3364] ....(3364) 2635

59) Ahaz (16) ....[3364-3379] ....(3379) 2620

--------------- 3 year overlap ---------------

60) Hezekiah (29)........[3377-3405] ....(3405) 2594

61) Manasseh (55)........[3405-3459] ....(3459) 2540

62) Amon (2)................[3459-3460]...............(3460).................2539

63) Josiah (31).............[3460-3490]...............(3490).................2509

64) Jehoahaz (3 months)[3490-3490]............(3490).................2509

65) Jehoiakim (11) ......[3490-3500]...............(3500).................2499

66) Jehoiachin (3 months)[3500-3500]..........(3500).................2499

67) Zedekiah (11)........[3500-3510]...............(3510).................2489

Next

The Babylonian Captivity

The Itemization of Time

NOTES

NOTES

The Itemization of Time

CHAPTER 7

THE BABYLONIAN CAPTIVITY

Mattaniah–Zedekiah was the final "King of Judah," <u>and not Israel</u>, to sit on the throne of "Judah" before the "Babylonian captivity." The "Kingdom of Israel" had been carried away into what was then, the Kingdom of Assyria by King Shalmaneser; after he laid siege on the Israelite capital city of Samaria 130 earlier. The Shalmaneser's siege itself lasted around three years. The period of the Babylonian Captivity was seventy years. The Prophet Jeremiah gave us his witness nineteen years earlier; saying to the peoples and to their wickedness, *"this whole land shall be a desolation, and an astonishment; and these nations shall serve the king of Babylon for seventy years"* (Jeremiah 25:1-<u>11</u>). Daniel would later confirm that Jeremiah wrote the prophecy (Daniel 9:2); as Daniel himself would experience the prophecy's precursory warning in

The Itemization of Time

the year 3500-3501 (*501-500 BC*) when Eliakim (Jehoiakim) was taken into Babylon with Daniel in tow. Daniel would also have to endure the complete duration of Jeremiah's prophecy's prime captivity from 3510-3580 (*491-421 BC*). Daniel was intimately too familiar with the truth and fulfillment of Jeremiah's 70 years prophecy about the desolations on/of Jerusalem. Therefore we have the years (*70*) and we have the proofs; which is the Holy Scripture record. From year 3510 (*491 BC*), we can continue the walk to do the math of accounting for biblical years; to discern, "*what time we are really in and how much time we have left.*"

The Event	Start and End of the Event	YHWH's Adamic Year	Ordained Time left
68) Babylon Captivity (70)	[3510-3580]	(3580)	2419

Next

Daniel's Seventy Weeks Prophecy

Timothy B. Merriman

NOTES

The Itemization of Time

NOTES

Timothy B. Merriman

CHAPTER 8

THE SEVENTY WEEKS PROPHECY

Not without issues and debates, the seventy weeks of Daniel covers the time period of the next 490 years after the destruction/desolation of the first temple that King Solomon constructed. Each day within Daniel's prophecy represents one complete literal year in the prophetic accounting of the ordained time for humans. Of course, the main controversy and complaint from the so-called *"experts"* of history and practically every reputable theologian concerning both my books' claims, would be their break-ups of Daniel's seventy week and the major conclusions because of those divisions. All of which, among other concerns are discussed in comprehensive and reasonable detail in my completed and overall thorough book of study and research, "**IT'S MUCH LATER THAN YOU THINK!**" It should be available online now; if not now, soon, wherever fine books are sold. So now, with all of its controversy, consider those divisions in Daniel's seventy weeks from the perspective of that book – from the end of the Jews Babylonian captivity in year 3580 (491 BC).

"The Seventy Weeks Divisions"

Jerusalem and the temple are rebuilt after **Seven (7) Weeks** or forty-nine (49) days/years

(Totals: 7 weeks)

The Event	Start and End of the Event	YHWH's Adamic Year	Ordained Time left
69) Rebuild temple (49)[3580-3629]		(3629)	2370

"Restore and to build Jerusalem;" and the temple. (Daniel 9:25)

Messiah is cut off (*crucified*) after **Threescore (60) Weeks** or (420) days/years **(Get the book!!)**

(Totals: 67 weeks)

The Event	Start and End of the Event	YHWH's Adamic Year	Ordained Time left
70) To the Crucifixion (420)[3629-4049]		(4049)	1951

"After threescore...weeks shall Messiah be cut off," (Daniel 9:26)

People of the prince will come after **Two (2) Weeks** or fourteen (14) days/years. In the name of the Prince's government a seven (7) year *private¿* and likely unofficial agreement or a covenant is struck with

The Itemization of Time

Jerusalem's influentials and the corrupt High Priest elected by Rome.

(Totals: 69 weeks)

The Event	Start and End of the Event	YHWH's Adamic Year	Ordained Time left

71) Prince's People (14)[4049-4063]..............(4063)................1937
"And after ~~threescore and~~ two weeks ~~shall Messiah be cut off, but not for himself; and~~ the people of the prince that [*] shall destroy the city and the sanctuary *[shall come];" (Daniel 9:26).

"Seven year treaty's two divisions"

Prince's people make a covenant with the High Priest and the influential seven (7) days/years.

"He confirms the covenant with many for one week"

After ½ week (3½) days/years - (The pledge/agreement/covenant is egregiously breached)

(Totals: 69 ½ weeks)

WAR BREAKS OUT!

The Event	Start and End of the Event	YHWH's Adamic Year	Ordained Time left

72) Jew/Rome War! (3½)[4063-4066.5].......(4066.5)............1933.5
"In the midst of the week he shall cause the sacrifice and the oblation to cease" (Daniel 9:27).

After (½) week, (3½) days/years the Jews lose the war with Rome; Jerusalem and her temple is in desolation. There is a claim that over a million Jews (*old and young*) are savagely slaughtered; with perhaps another 100 thousand made slaves. It was as Yeshua and Daniel prophesied. By this infamous event in Jewish history, Rome's tsunami of destruction, mayhem and murder was their retaliation and ultimate spiritual insult against the insolent Jews and their God. At the site of the temple, not one stone was left upon another. **(Totals: 70 weeks)**

The Event	Start and End of the Event	YHWH's Adamic Year	Ordained Time left
73) Jews defeated (3½)[4066.5-4070]		(4070)	1930

"...*and the end thereof...with a flood*" (Daniel 9:26)

The Itemization of Time

NOTES

NOTES

The Itemization of Time

CHAPTER 9

THE BC/AD CORRESPONDING CHART

The list years below correspond to the list years above in numerical sequence; i.e. 1), 2), 3) to show the equivalent BC/AD determinations (Lived/Died) of YHWH's Adamic years referenced; so readers might discern YHWH's Adamic years in BC/AD or its alternative BCE/CE terms and perhaps gain insights to why Messiah, Yeshua or *"Jesus Christ's"* date to appear is not yet on us. Being able to visually see and compare BC/AD conversions to YHWH's Adamic years, can be a key when relating to or in revealing **_what time we are really in and how much time we have left_**.

Name	Age/Years	Lived/Died
1) Adam created	(*)	(4000 BC)
2) Adam	(930 age)	(4000-3070 BC)

The Itemization of Time

3) Seth .... (912 age) .... (3870-2958 BC)

4) Enos .... (905 age) .... (3765-2860 BC)

5) Cainan .... (910 age) .... (3675-2765 BC)

6) Mahalaleel .... (895 age) .... (3605-2710 BC)

7) Jared .... (962 age) .... (3540-2578 BC)

8) Enoch (Translated) .... (365 age) .... (3378-3013 BC)

9) Methuselah .... (969 age) .... (3313-2344 BC)

10) Lamech .... (777 age) .... (3126-2349 BC)

11) Noah .... (950 age) .... (2944-1994 BC)

12) Shem .... (603 age) .... (2444-1843 BC)

13) Arphaxad .... (428 age) .... (2341-1913 BC)

14) Salah .... (433 age) .... (2316-1883 BC)

15) Eber .... (456 age) .... (2286-1830 BC)

16) Peleg .... (239 age) .... (2260-2021 BC)

17) Reu .... (235 age) .... (2230-1995 BC)

18) Serug .... (230 age) .... (2202-1972 BC)

19) Nahor .... (130 age) .... (2172-2042 BC)

20) Te' rah .... (205 age) .... (2161-1956 BC)

21) Abram/Abraham .... (175 age) .... (2111-1936 BC)

22) Isaac .... (180 age) .... (2011-1831 BC)

23) Jacob/Israel .... (130 age) .... (**To Egypt**-1821 BC)

24) Israel left Egypt .... (430 yrs) .... (1821-1391 BC)

25) Wilderness of Sin .... (40 yrs) .... (1391-1351 BC)

Judges and the Adversary

26) king Chushan .... (8 yrs) .... (1350-1343 BC)

27) **Judge Othniel** .... (40 yrs) .... (1342-1303 BC)

28) king Eglon .... (18 yrs) .... (1302-1285 BC)

29) **Judge Ehud** .... (80 yrs) .... (1284-1205 BC)

30) king Jabin .... (20 yrs) .... (1204-1185 BC)

31) **Judge Deborah** .... (40 yrs) .... (1184-1145 BC)

32) Midianites .... (7 yrs) .... (1144-1138 BC)

33) **Judge Gideon** .... (40 yrs) .... (1137-1098 BC)

34) Abimelech .... (3 yrs) .... (1097-1095 BC)

35) **Judge Tola** .... (23 yrs) .... (1094-1072 BC)

36) **Judge Jair** .... (22 yrs) .... (1071-1050 BC)

37) Philistines .... (18 yrs) .... (1049-1032 BC)

38) **Judge Jephthah** .... (6 yrs) .... (1031-1026 BC)

39) **Judge Ibzan** .... (7 yrs) .... (1025-1019 BC)

40) **Judge Elon** .... (10 yrs) .... (1018-1009 BC)

The Itemization of Time

41) **Judge Abdon** ....(8 yrs).......................(1008-1001 BC)

42) Philistines.........................(40 yrs).......................(1000-961 BC)

43) **Judge Sampson** ....(20 yrs)..........................(960-941 BC)

The United States of Israel

44) King David (Net yrs) ....(26 yrs)..........................(940-915 BC)

45) King Solomon...................(40 yrs)..........................(914-875 BC)

Kings of Judah

46) Rehoboam.........................(17 yrs)..........................(874-858 BC)

47) Abijam ....(3 yrs)............................(857-855 BC)

48) Asa ....(41 yrs)..........................(855-815 BC)

49) Jehoshaphat......................(25 yrs)..........................(815-791 BC)

50) Jehoram............................(8 yrs)............................(794-787 BC)

51) Ahaziah............................(1 yrs)............................(788-788 BC)

52) Athaliah (woman) ....(7 yrs)............................(789-781 BC)

53) Joash/Jehoash...................(40 yrs)..........................(781-742 BC)

54) Amaziah...........................(29 yrs)..........................(744-716 BC)

55) Uzziah/Azariah ....(52 yrs)..........................(704-653 BC)

56) Jotham..............................(16 yrs)..........................(652-637 BC)

57) Ahaz ....(16 yrs)..........................(637-622 BC)

58) Hezekiah ....(29 yrs)........................(624-596 BC)

59) Manasseh ....(55 yrs)........................(596-542 BC)

60) Amon ....(2 yrs)..........................(542-541 BC)

61) Josiah ....(31 yrs)........................(541-511 BC)

62) Jehoahaz ....(3 months) ....(511-511 BC)

63) Eliakim/Jehoiakim ....(11 yrs)........................(511-501 BC)

64) Jehoiachin......................(3 months) ....(501-501 BC)

65) Mattaniah/Zedekiah ....(11 yrs)........................(501-491 BC)

66) **Babylon Captivity** ....(70 yrs)........................(491-421 BC)

Daniel's Seventy Weeks Prophecy (W = weeks)

67) Second Temple (7**W**).......(49 yrs)........................(421-372 BC)

68) **Messiah cut off** (60**W**)...(420 yrs) ....(372 BC-**AD 49**)

69) Covenant (2**W**) ....(14 yrs).....................(AD 49 - AD 63)

70) **War!** (1/2**W**) ....(3 ½ yrs)...............(AD 63 - **AD 66 ½**)

71) **Jews defeated** (1/2**W**)....(3 ½ yrs)...............(AD 66 ½ - **AD 70**)

The Itemization of Time

NOTES

Timothy B. Merriman

NOTES

The Itemization of Time

CHAPTER 10

WHAT HAPPENS NEXT?

For those who might have noticed it, the accounting of time in this booklet has stopped at YHWH's Adamic/Hebrew year of 4070. For those who might not recognize where we are at, the base year 4070 is equivalent to our Gregorian AD 70. To translate any AD number from YHWH Adamic/Hebrew Calendar, one merely needs to subtract 4000 years from any number referenced above 4000. If that number is below 4000 – just subtract 4001. <u>This is due to the fact there is no zero year between BC and AD</u>. Yes, you will initially get a negative number. Discard the negative you get before the number and add BC, BCE or my personal favorite, BMB (*Before Messiah Birth*) after the number and you now have the transformation date.

<u>What happens next</u>? At the place in time where we have paused

at (*AD 70*); we still have theoretically and from my perspective theologically, 1931 years remaining until "Jesus" is said to imply he would return. That is based on the "Millennial Week" and "Millennial Reign" preached in many churches across this nation and the world. But, "SNAP!" Wait a deceived minute! When I add 1931 years to AD 70, I come to AD 2001! (**REALLY!¿?**) Did not we pass that date around twenty (20) years ago - in our reality of counting the time? I have another question for everyone.

"Why, seeing times are not hidden from the Almighty, do they that know him not see his days?"(**Job 24:1**)

In other and rearranged words, "If we say we know him, we should have his Spirit. And we know the Spirit searches out the deep things of YHWH. (1st Corinthians 2:10) Our condition is rather unique. Seeing times are not laid up and hidden from YHWH's Spirit, why can't we see his days? And if we possibly can, why would not that last day be included? I guess that is several questions that I have asked, instead of the initial one I claimed. You have my apologies. But, the facts remain. There is a challenge that we should see his days – especially we who have come to see these "***last minutes***" of the last day before Yeshua returns. Daniel prophesies in the last days *"knowledge shall be increased"* (12:4) and *"the wise shall understand"* (Verse 10). If we do not understand, what does it *truly* say about us and our so-called *relationship* with "*Jesus Christ?*"

1) "*Jesus Christ*" promised he would shorten the days, so why are we sitting at 6019?
   a. A Millennial Week is 7000 years.
   b. The Millennial Reign was supposed to have started at the beginning of year 6001.
   c. **4000** years BC (Plus) **AD 2020** years (Equals) 6020 years. Something is not right!

2) If "*Jesus Christ*" did not shorten the days, does that make "*Jesus Christ*" a liar?

3) Does the Holy Bible reveal who the Antichrist is?

4) Does the Holy Bible reveal when we can expect the Antichrist to appear?

5) When will the third temple be built and does the Holy Bible reveal it?

I believe these are all legitimate questions that we as believers should be able to answer. I believe the reasons we do not know these things is because we lack wisdom on these matters and have not asked for the wisdom to answer them truthfully, to our spiritual satisfaction. I did ask! I believed the promise of YHWH our Eloah. Hear from Ya'akov (*James*) and then Shaul (*Paul*).

> "If any of you lack wisdom, let him ask of God, that giveth to all *men* liberally, and upbraideth not; and it shall be given him. But let him ask in faith, nothing wavering: for he that wavereth is like a wave of the sea driven with the wind and tossed. For let not that man think that he shall receive any thing of the Lord" (James 1:5-7).

> "...because that which may be known of God is manifest in them; for God hath showed it unto them. For the invisible things of him from the creation of the world are clearly seen, being understood by the things that are made" (Romans 1:19-20)

Here and now - I assert YHWH has shown me important information regarding prophecy in the end time. I have written concerning many of those things, including some questions I listed and asked YHWH above in the book entitled, <u>IT'S MUCH LATER THAN YOU THINK!</u> There is no doubt; my book will be a challenging and controversial read. Usually, most new or revealed knowledge is. This booklet is merely a condensed outline of some of the information YHWH has revealed to me. I have not contended to explain the mindset in which YHWH had to place me in, to be able to receive discernment from his Holy Spirit. That is a book within itself. Maybe I will perhaps write it one day. Notwithstanding, YHWH has many last day and last minute mysteries to unveil; if I may call them that. From my perspective, some are offered up for your study in the book <u>IT'S MUCH LATER THAN YOU THINK!</u> They are clarified with plain and divine logic.

If you don't have that book, I encourage you to get you a copy as soon as you can. If you are reading this section as part of that book; then, you already know a lot in answers to my list of questions above and more. Nevertheless, there were some matters concerning certain issues that I could not write – even in that book. But – after you have read that book – if you think you would like to know, ***"The rest of the story"*** (Paul Harvey); I encourage you to write to me then, for that information. I am now presently in the processes of getting that information in written form. I am ashamed to say we will need your aid when you write to us; to help cover the costs of getting that word out to you. Sadly, I am not saying anything you do not already know. You know thing cost <u>a lot</u> today. I don't have a large church tithing in order to be able to send out this ought-to-be-free information free-of-charge. I ask for you to pray for our group that YHWH will forgive us in this transgression, *which it is*; because I did not have to pay to get it. But please, send $14.95 or more if the Spirit inspires - with your request for the information, "*Article of Omission*." If you cannot, we will still do what we can for as long as we can. Well now, I'd say that's enough begging for now.

As for the more essential book "<u>IT'S MUCH LATER THAN YOU THINK!</u>" it should be available at Amazon, Barnes and Nobles or wherever free speech is welcome. Finally, we vow to keep "*Article of Omission*" openly available for long as we can. I say this because of my concern over the two beasts. Not in their coming. They are already here! Their relentless efforts to silence free speech in reality are not set up to shut up its political enemy. That type victory would merely be the proverbial icing on its cake. In truth its real target is the assemblies of Yeshua. The beasts' ultimate goal is evident. They want the unadulterated Gospel of Eloah's Kingdom silenced. You will understand better once you have read the book, <u>IT'S MUCH LATER THAN YOU THINK!</u>

The premise of the book, "<u>IT'S MUCH LATER THAN YOU THINK!</u>" and this booklet that you have now almost completely read, "<u>The Itemization of Time;</u>" I contend that they are both based on two biblically sound doctrines. The first doctrine being; that YHWH has an ordained time for man's self-rule. My study has led me to think and conclude that this "ordained time" is found in shadow picture throughout the entirety of the Holy Scriptures. One study focus in coming to this doctrine would be the established biblical feast of YHWH. It is mainly recognized in the western hemisphere as <u>The Feast of Tabernacles</u>. It is a gathering for the temporary dwelling; signifying man's temporary dwelling here on the earth in his carnal flesh. Without a drawn out study being conducted here, <u>The Feast of Tabernacles</u> is a physical seven-day observance; also signifying in its shadow picture, YHWH millennial week (**<u>7000 years</u>**), for man to run his own show after he rejected YHWH's authority over him in the Garden of Eden. Man's time is 6000 years; add to it Yeshua's Millennial Reign. The second doctrine, of which I am dogmatic about, is the certainty that Yeshua said and so he will shorten the days or we would destroy ourselves (Matthew 24:22).

So, our query quandary, our grim gridlock, our immovable impasse, our doctrinal disaster and our theological at-a-loss seems to be this very thought-provoking jewel for its prize. Looking ahead from AD 70, which corresponds to YHWH's Adamic year of 4070; when we add the 1931 years to the overall 7000 years premise - the years I maintain we have left on the millennial week before a Messiah is expected to come - *or closer to my own belief, his return*; we come not to the immediate present or to the near future, not even to the far future, as far as time is concerned. But indeed we come to the past, the year of AD 2001. This is equivalent in many Messianic circles to the year 6001. With its equally distasteful alternative, when we gander ahead a second time from AD 70, where we unceremoniously halted; many Christians today contend or believe that we live in AD 2020 or else they must confess - *much to their chagrin* - they do not have any idea what-so-ever of what time it really is as to what time we are living in. With AD 2020 determined by most to be correct, it appears that they agree with several Messianic groups and believers that the real Jewish year is supposedly 6019. If so-called sober minded Christians were to accept such a premise, we would have to also confess we past year 6001 two decades ago. If this is the understanding

The Itemization of Time

we posses, it is faith-breaking apparent, there was no shortening of the days. But indeed, it appears there was a lengthening of the days *"Jesus Christ"* promised to shorten. I will quote *"Jesus"* for convenience. "...*those days* **shall be** *shortened*" (Matthew 24:22). How can it be then? I mean how can we find ourselves in year 6019 (*AD 2020*) and no "Jesus?" Did he change his mind or something? Citing a premise, did he take us off the 7000 year millennial week and cast us into the unknown aspects of time. Did *Jesus* do this and simply neglected to tell his prophets of the change? For *Jesus*, that is out of spirit.

If these accusations are true, it could be argued such actions makes *"Jesus"* a liar! Consider these Bible passages. "*Surely the Lord God will do nothing, but he revealeth his secret unto his servants the prophets*" (Amos 3:7) or, "*Heaven and earth shall pass away, but my words shall not pass away*" (Matthew 24:35). And you can take this to the bank. Heaven and earth have not passed away. That I know. I spied them out just a moment ago. Since heaven and earth are still here, we have to seriously consider this real dilemma. When it comes to the truth, a lie or simply our misunderstanding, at whose feet do we lay the error? The sober spiritual mind must conclude the fault exists in our understanding. If we judge and compare spiritual possibilities, probabilities and non-repercussion (*being heaven and earth are still here*), there is only one option that does not stinks to high heaven. <u>Most (**_you_**)</u> **do not know** <u>what time it really is and how much time we have left</u>. **6019 and AD 2020 has to be off somehow**. Or else, why did not *Jesus* return **19 years ago**? Since no one else has bothered to down this <u>Demonic Bull</u> in the Christian China Shop, I took dead aim; before it is able to do what some might term as irreparable damage. When we see the faith of many today, we would have to conclude, some damage has already been done. You will need the complement of this book to find out the shocking truths which still eludes your spiritual discernment and is ready to be revealed. Don't let anybody fool you. <u>IT'S MUCH LATER THAN YOU THINK</u>!

The Itemization of Time

NOTES

NOTES

NOTES

Timothy B. Merriman

References

Smithsonian Institute, (2019). "Introduction to Human Evolution." *The Smithsonian Institution's Human Origins Program*. The Smithsonian Institute, 16 Jan. 2019.

http://humanorigins.si.edu/education/introduction-human-evolution.

Timothy B. Merriman

WHO IS TIMOTHY B. MERRIMAN? (*Continued from back - 3*)

"If I may say so, the past forty-five years has not been a proverbial, "*pillar of success*," spiritual wise. If any of my friends were to be as kind so to call my life a, "*shining star;*" I do not have to imagine. One would need something much more powerful than the Hubble Telescope to be able to view my light over against the night sky. I wager you get the gist; which leaves one begging to question. Why would our Eloah - *YHWH Elohim* - trust a person like me with the distribution of, **The Bridge to Prophecy**? [*Not my words*] In three words; I don't know. But, here I am. Here you are. And absolutely, judgment and time will tell the story concerning the level of truth contained in the set of my two books, "The Itemization of Time;" then, "IT'S MUCH LATER THAN YOU THINK!" In my study of biblical time, they lay out for you my odyssey to prophetic discovery.

WHO IS TIMOTHY B. MERRIMAN? (*Continued from back - 2*)

thrown upon, I felt like my spiritual life went through "All of that!" As soon as you can, study on the parable yourself. I believe some of you will empathize with my plight as it might possibly reflect on some events and experiences in your own lives.

With my Bible knowledge being less than stellar, I had to learn pretty much from scratch. I had questions about the Bible. I went to people I thought knew; i.e. pastors and preachers. Sad to say, I found in most cases that was a mistake. If the Bible said a thing contrary to their denomination, they chose denomination over Bible every time. In the rare case when one did side with the Bible over their denomination, they valued their pastoral position or statuses as spiritual pillars in their churches and communities over what I will call "bible controversy;" and so, were afraid to speak out with their perceived enlightenment. Growing up in America at age 15, it was safe to say I had and have no Hebrew roots to speak of; so temptations were victorious over me; *if you know what I mean.* And I don't need to speak of the many distractions the world offers to steal our attention away from God. But I thank YHWH - *in my latter years* - I can finally relate to the good ground.

The Itemization of Time

WHO IS TIMOTHY B. MERRIMAN? (*Continued from back - 1*)

At age 15 you can be assured that I knew everything there was to know about God and the Holy Bible – **NOT!** But, at age 15 – you can easily imagine I thought that I did. In actuality, I doubt if in a biblical quiz, I would have been able to recite the Ten Commandments. That was the truth. I did not have an abundance of Holy Bible knowledge, but, "The **LORD**" had infused me – *I think* – with wisdom and social insight past my years. I think he does that with a lot of people he calls. But then, as we all should know, "*Many are called...*" "*...but few are chosen*" (Matthew 22:14).

I would like to think only the individuals themselves can tell you what that is like; but, we have a witness from the Holy Scripture that describes the situation quite brilliantly. It is in the words of Messiah in his parable of the sower (Luke 8:4-15). If you have never read it, take the time to do so at your earliest convenience. I would liken myself at that time to the parable's *Alladat* ground. No - *Alladat* is not a Hebrew, Greek or Arabic word. What do you mean, "THEN THERE'S NO <u>ALLADAT</u> GROUND?" Alladat may not be a Hebrew, Arabic or Greek word, but it is mine – I made it up; because that is precisely how I fertilized out. You see, when Messiah spoke to all of the grounds his seed (*the WORD*) was

www.ingramcontent.com/pod-product-compliance
Lightning Source LLC
LaVergne TN
LVHW041633070426
835507LV00008B/602